Coolerbooks

ISBN:1523346175
ISBN-13:9781523346172

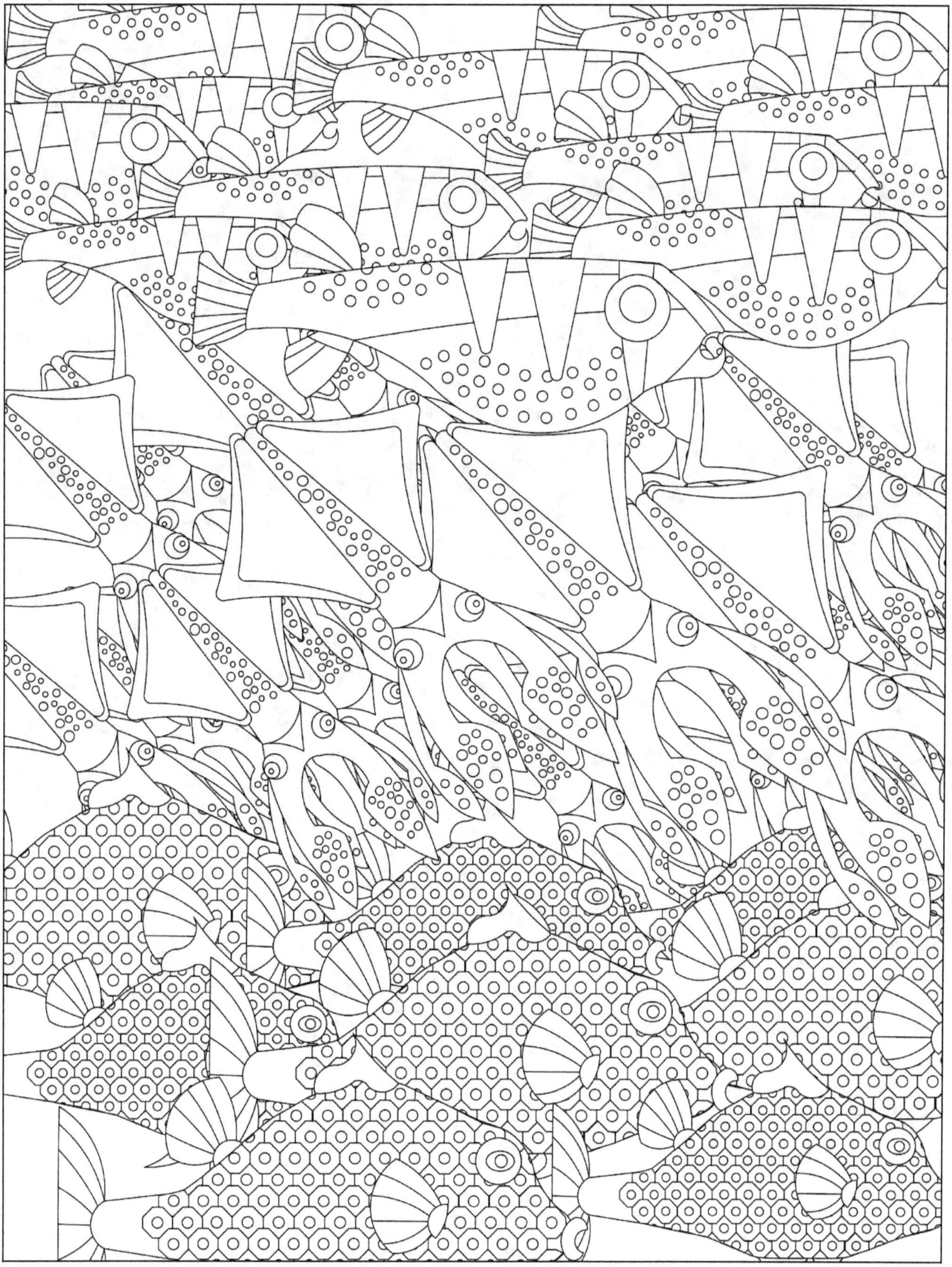

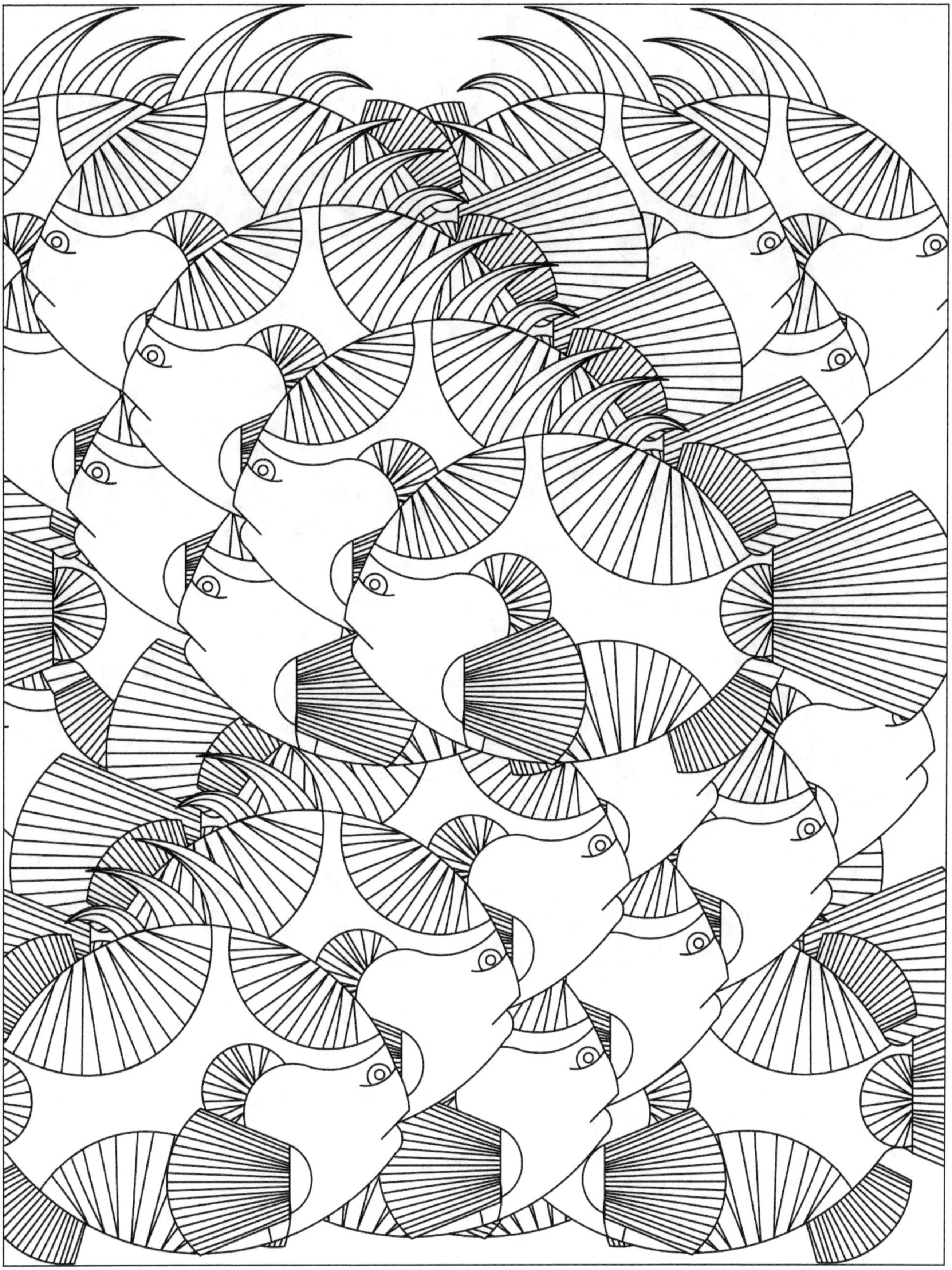

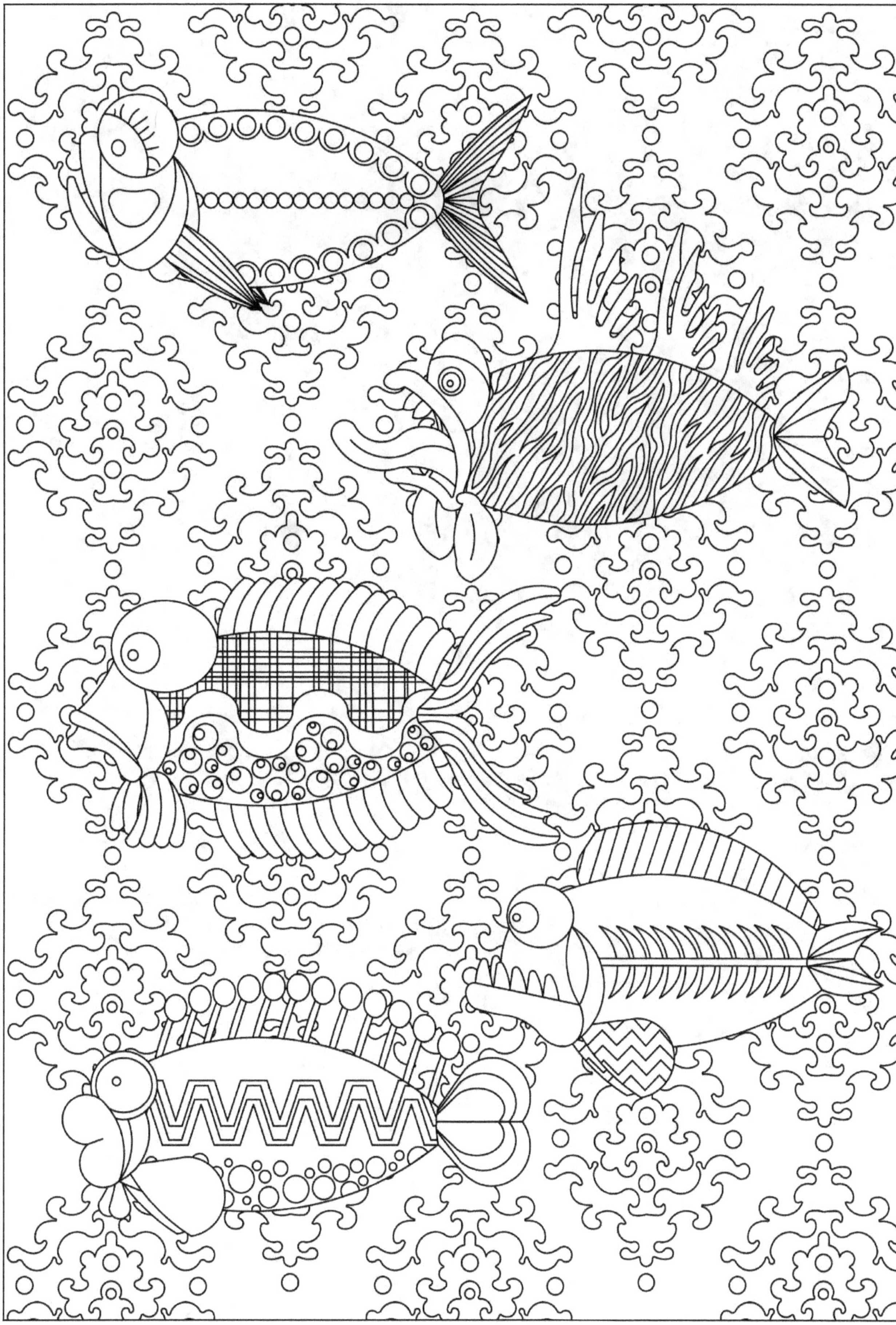

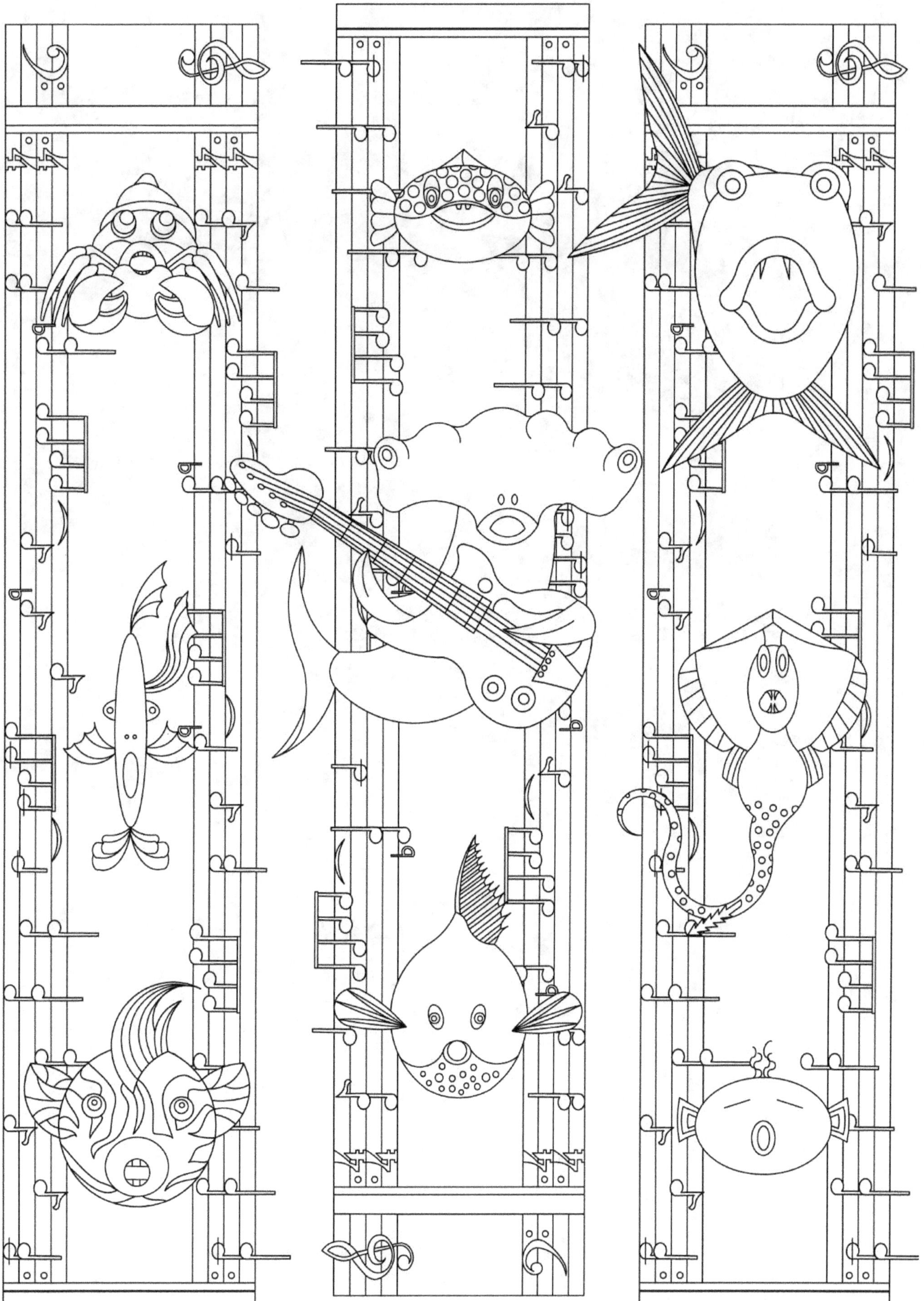

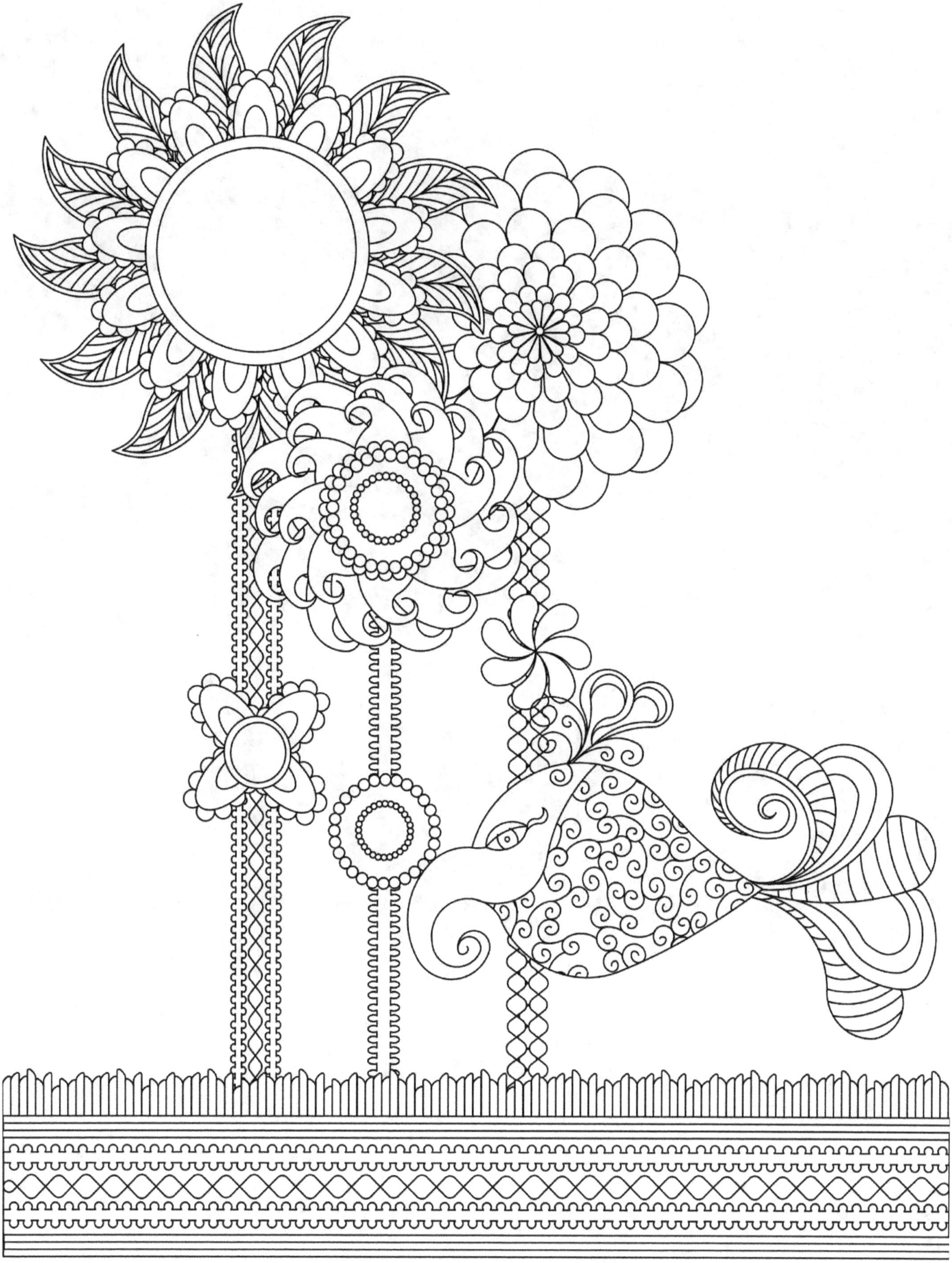

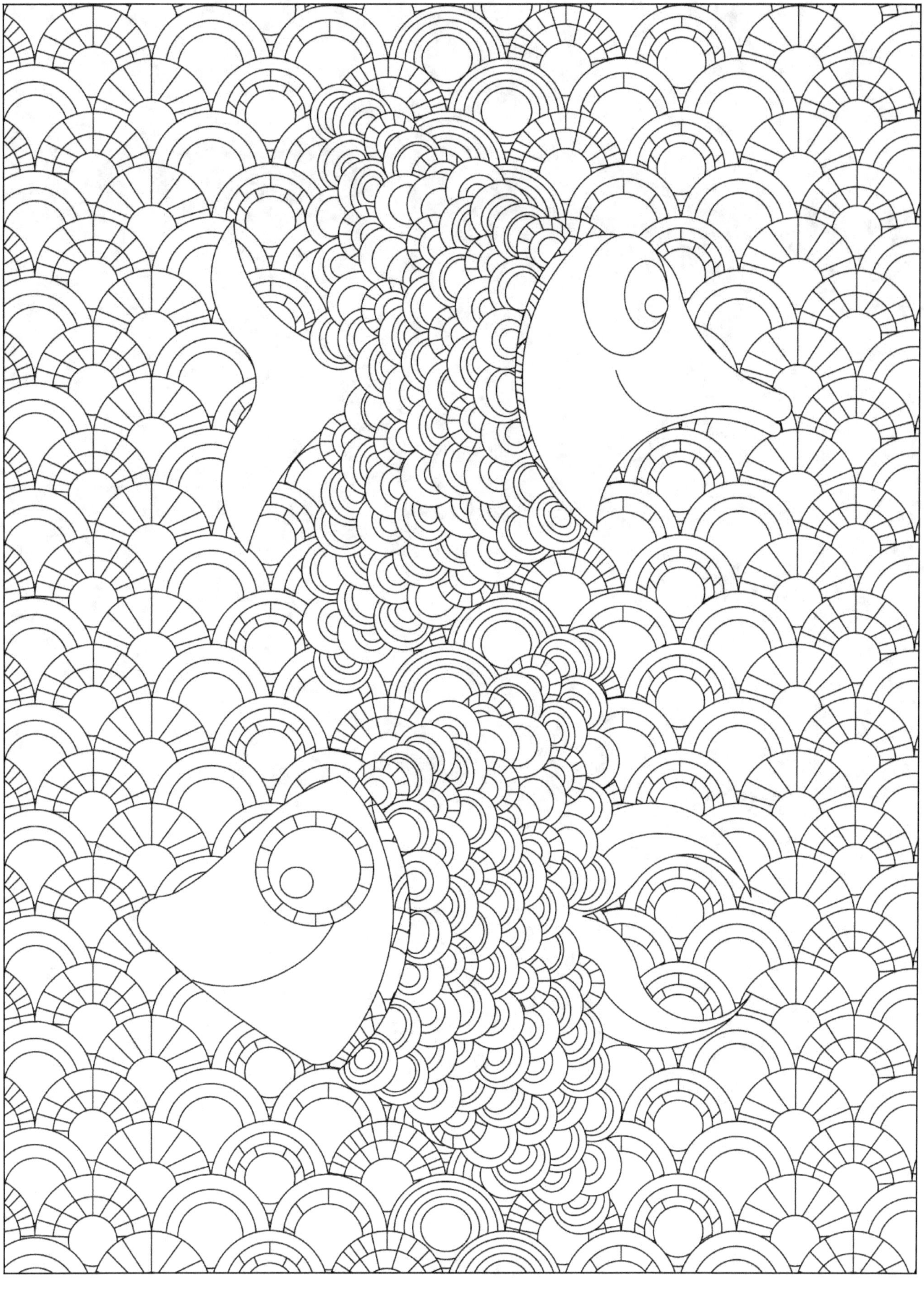

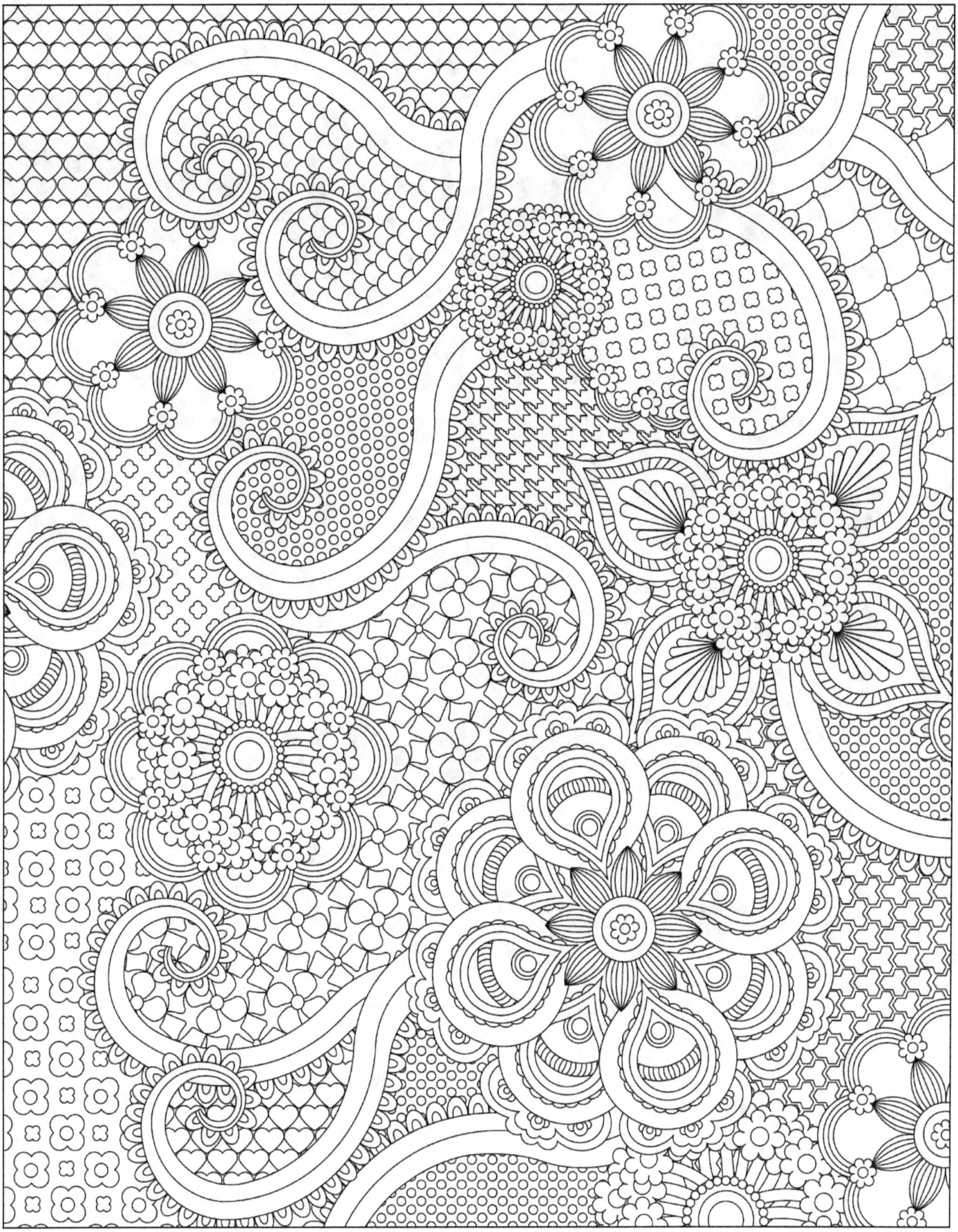

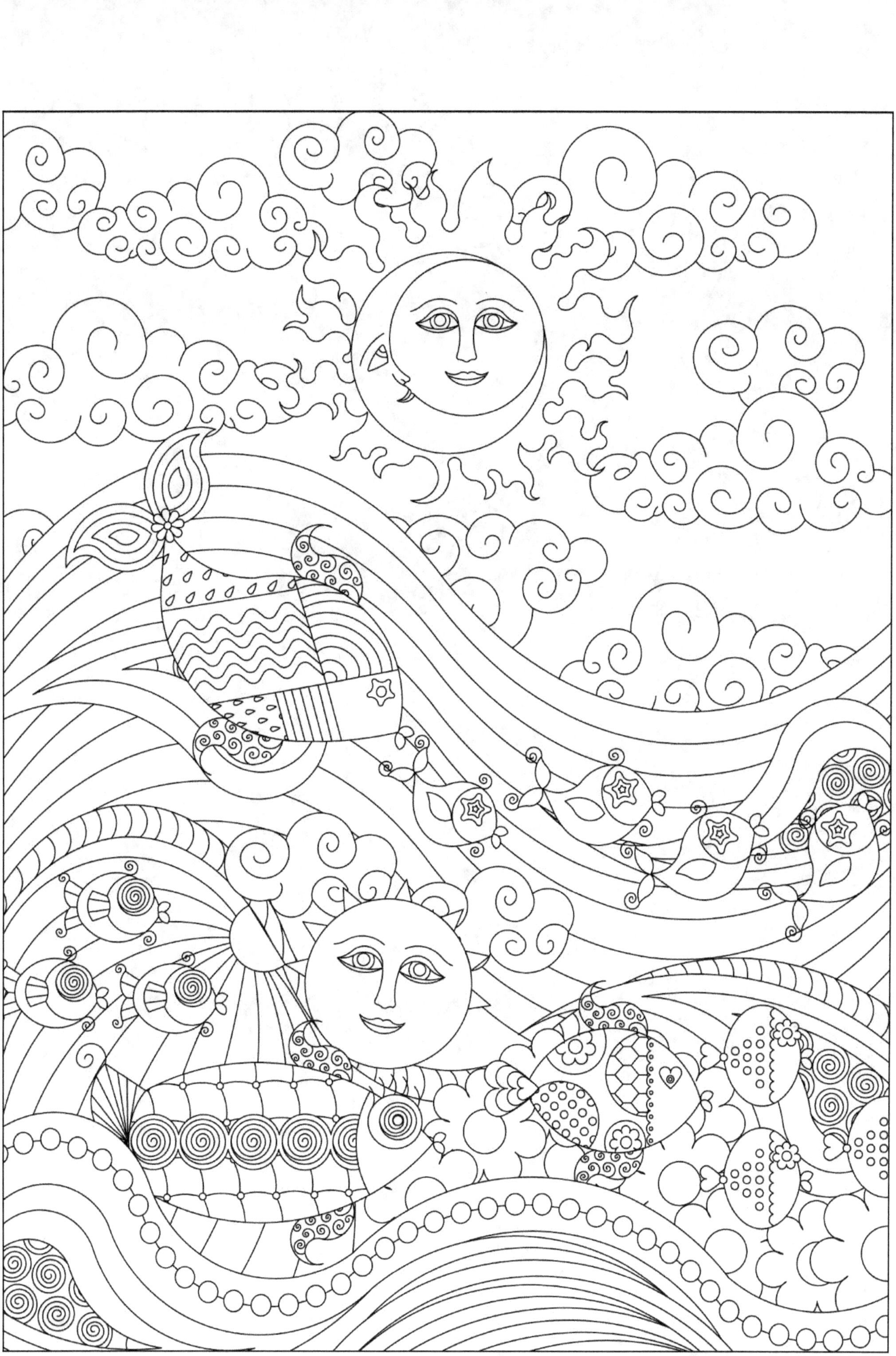

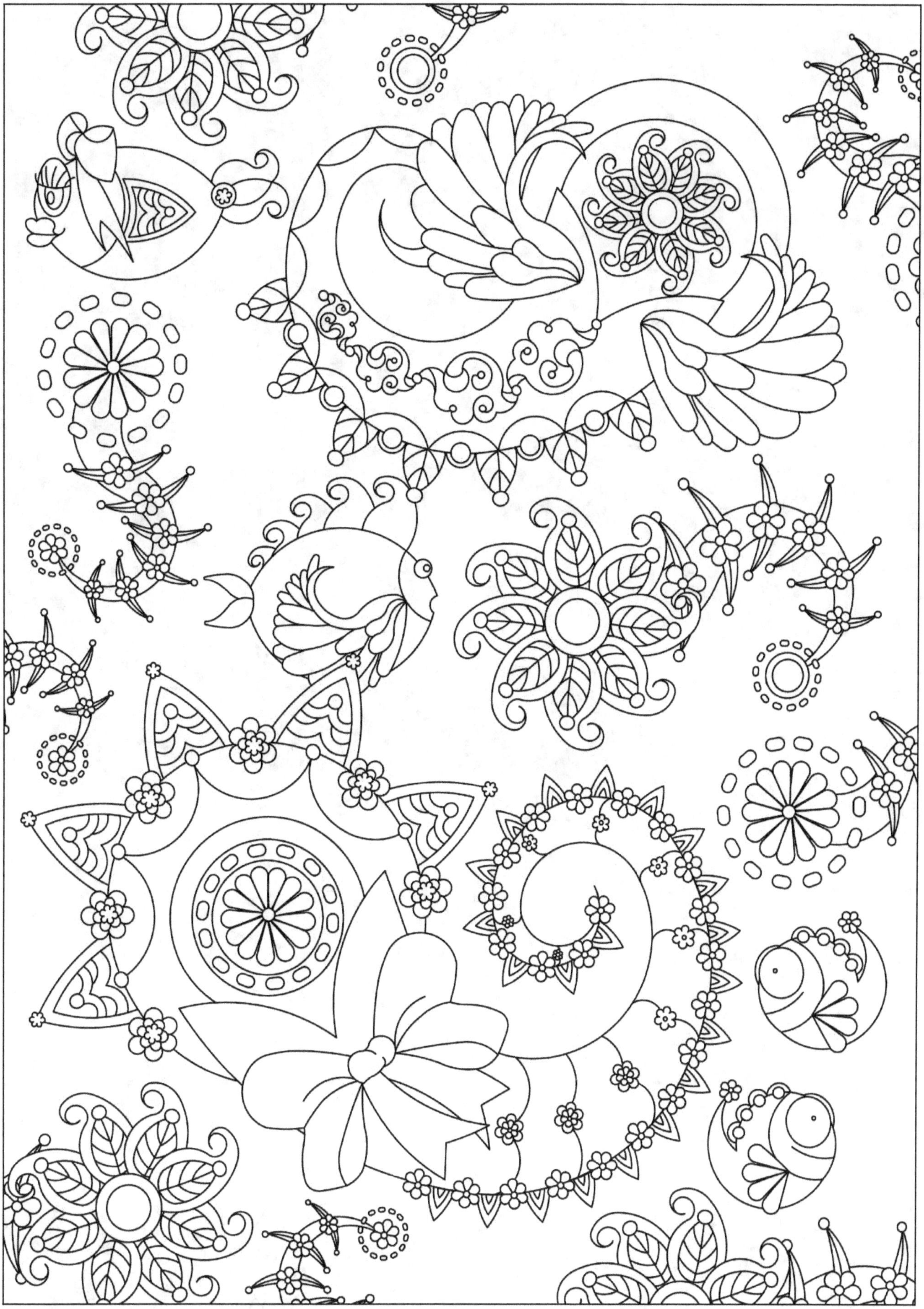

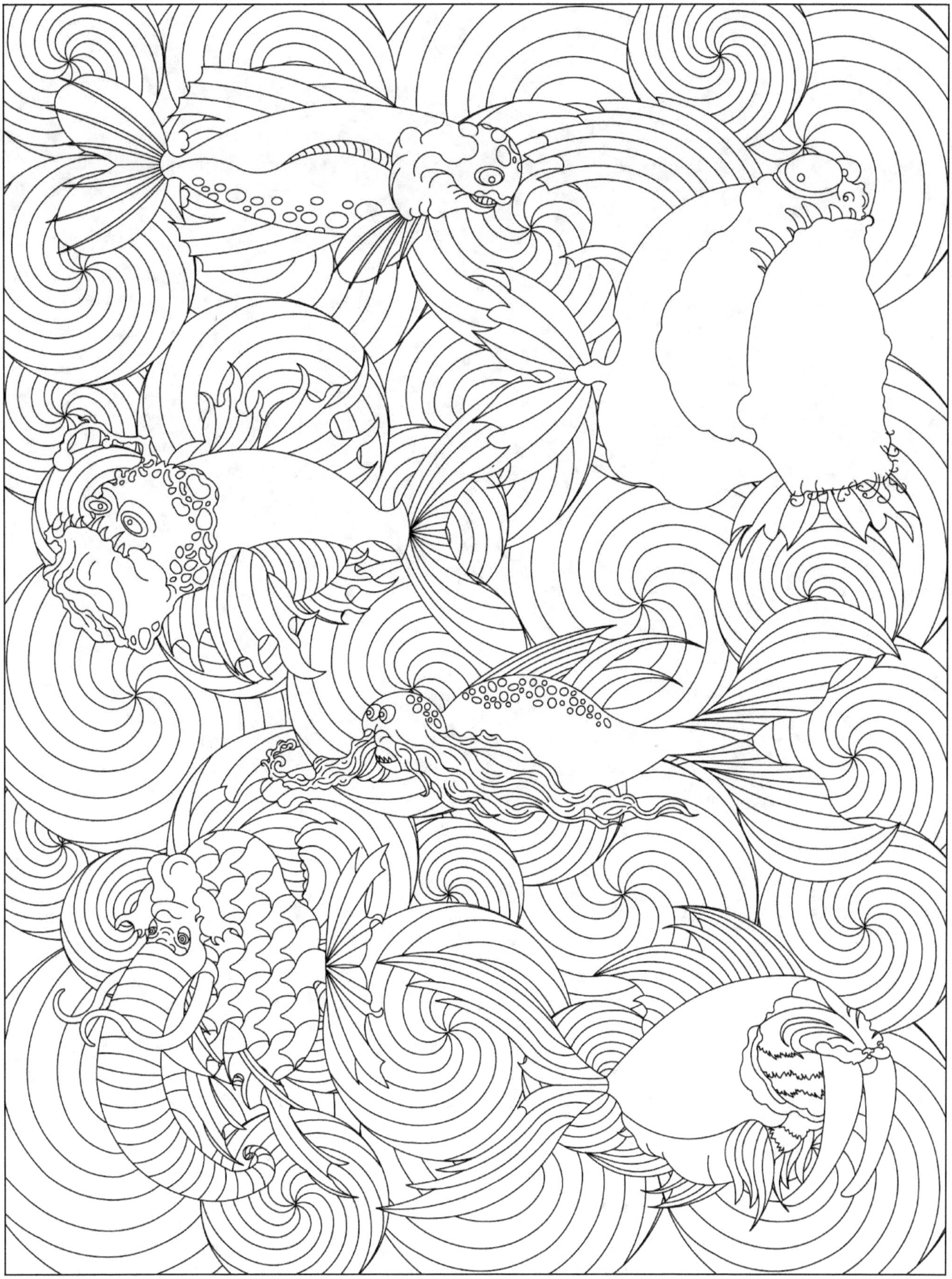

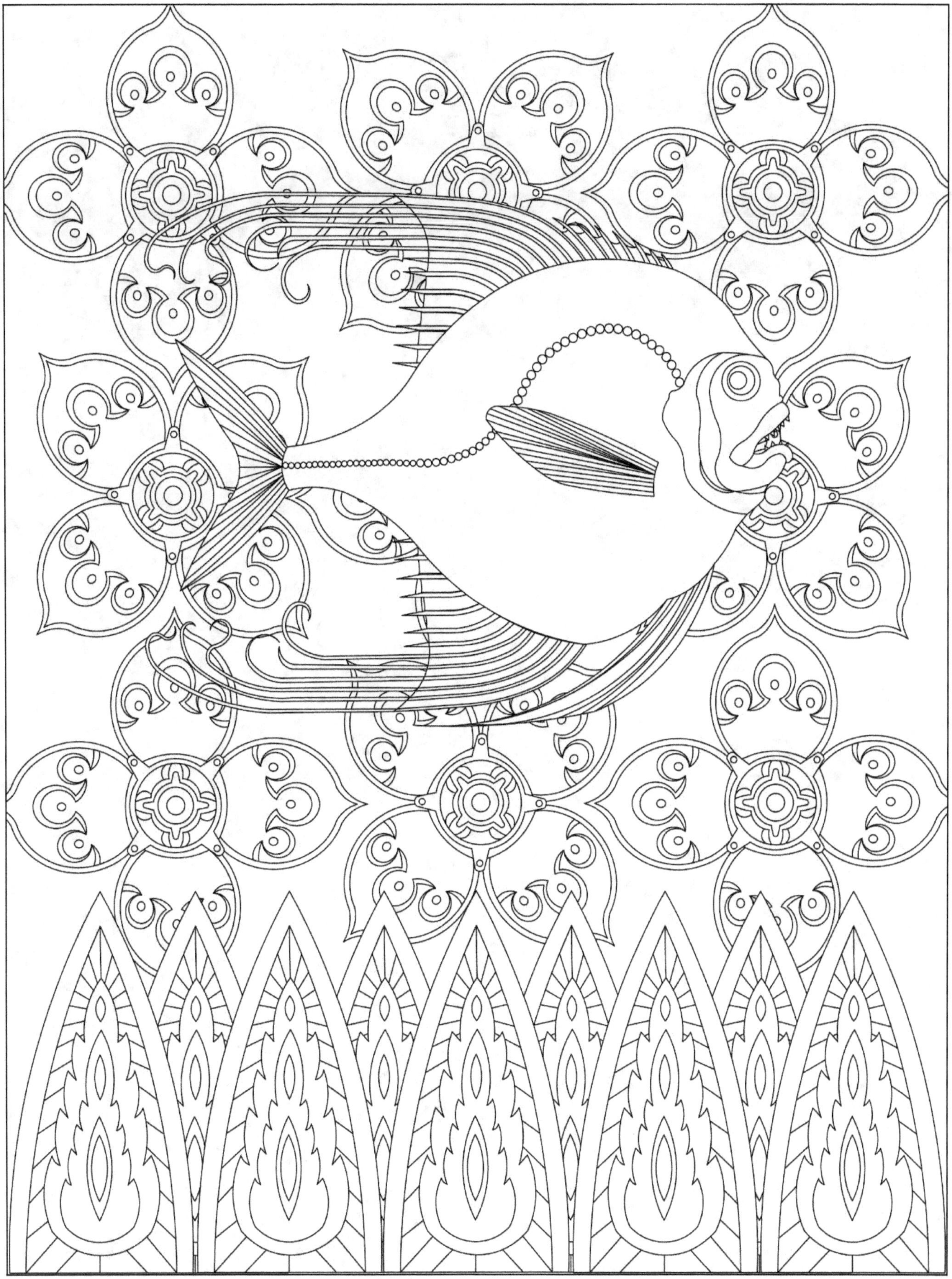

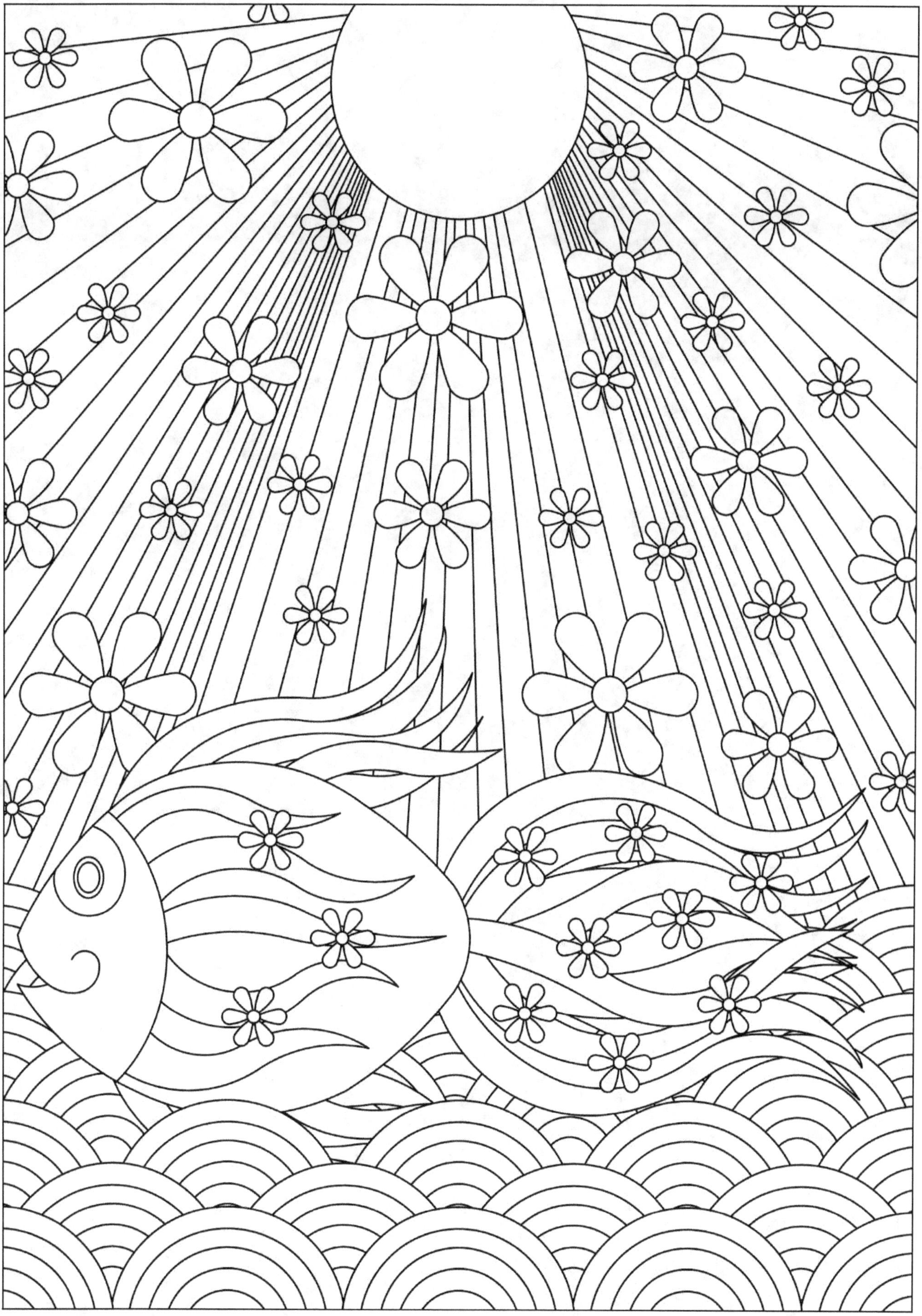

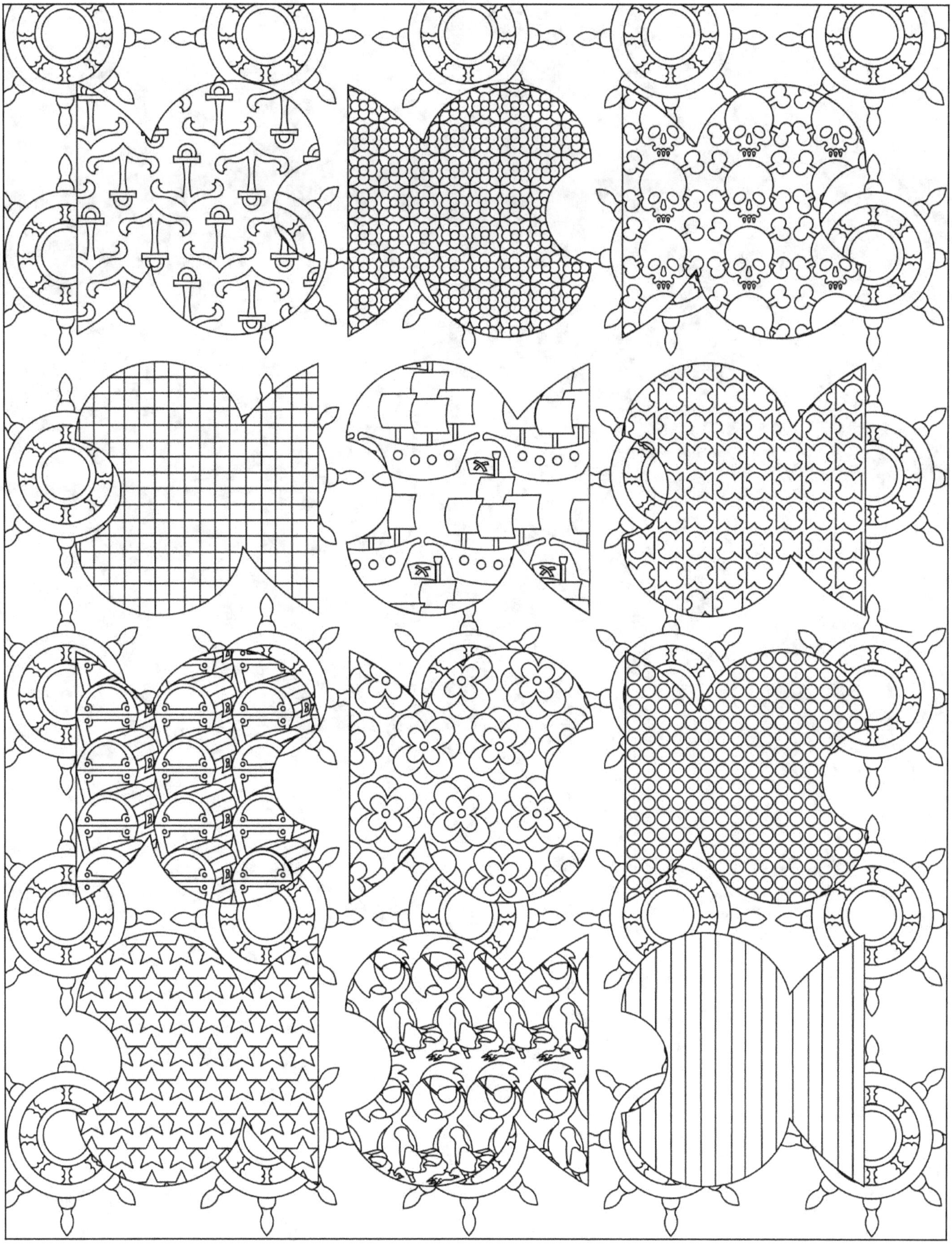

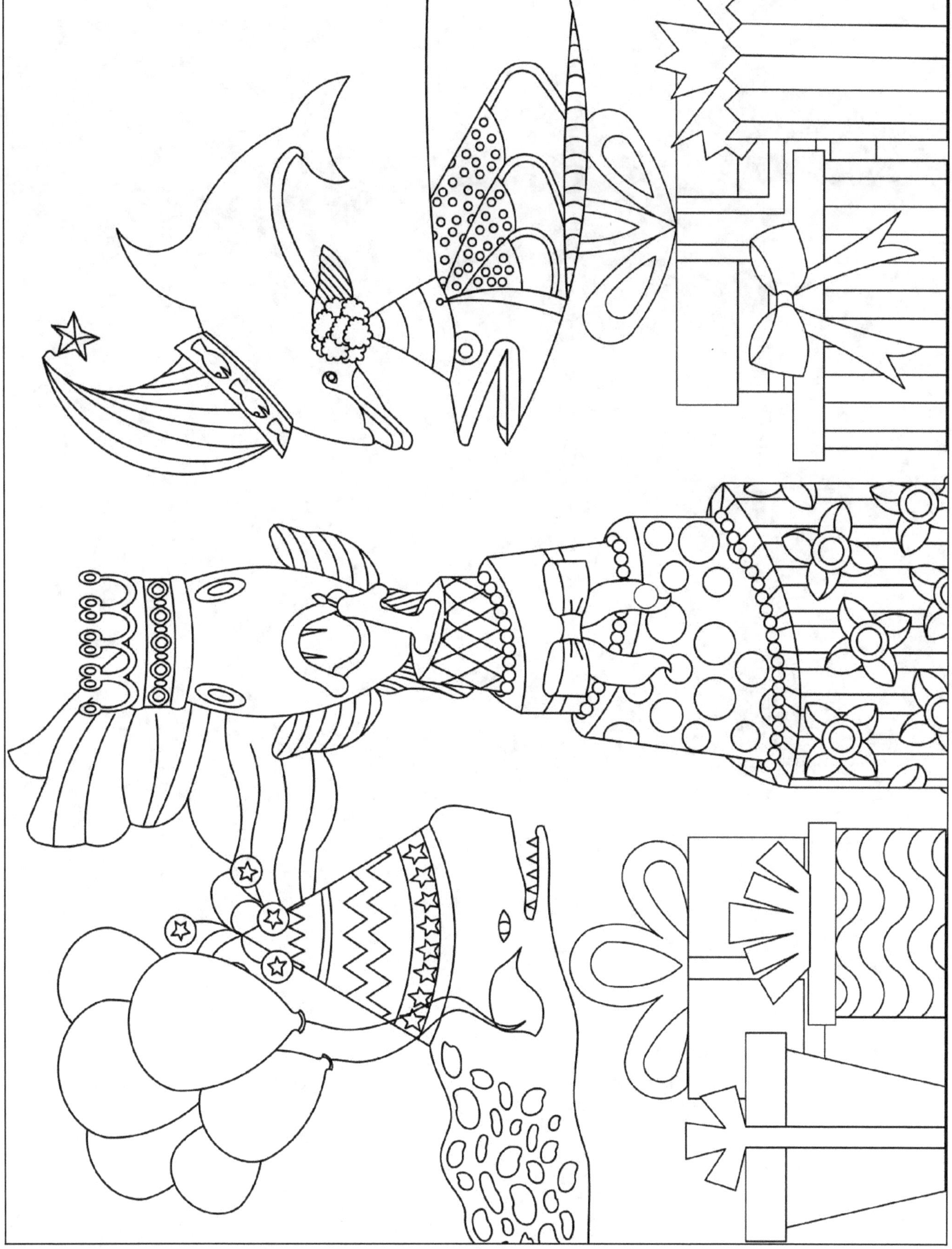

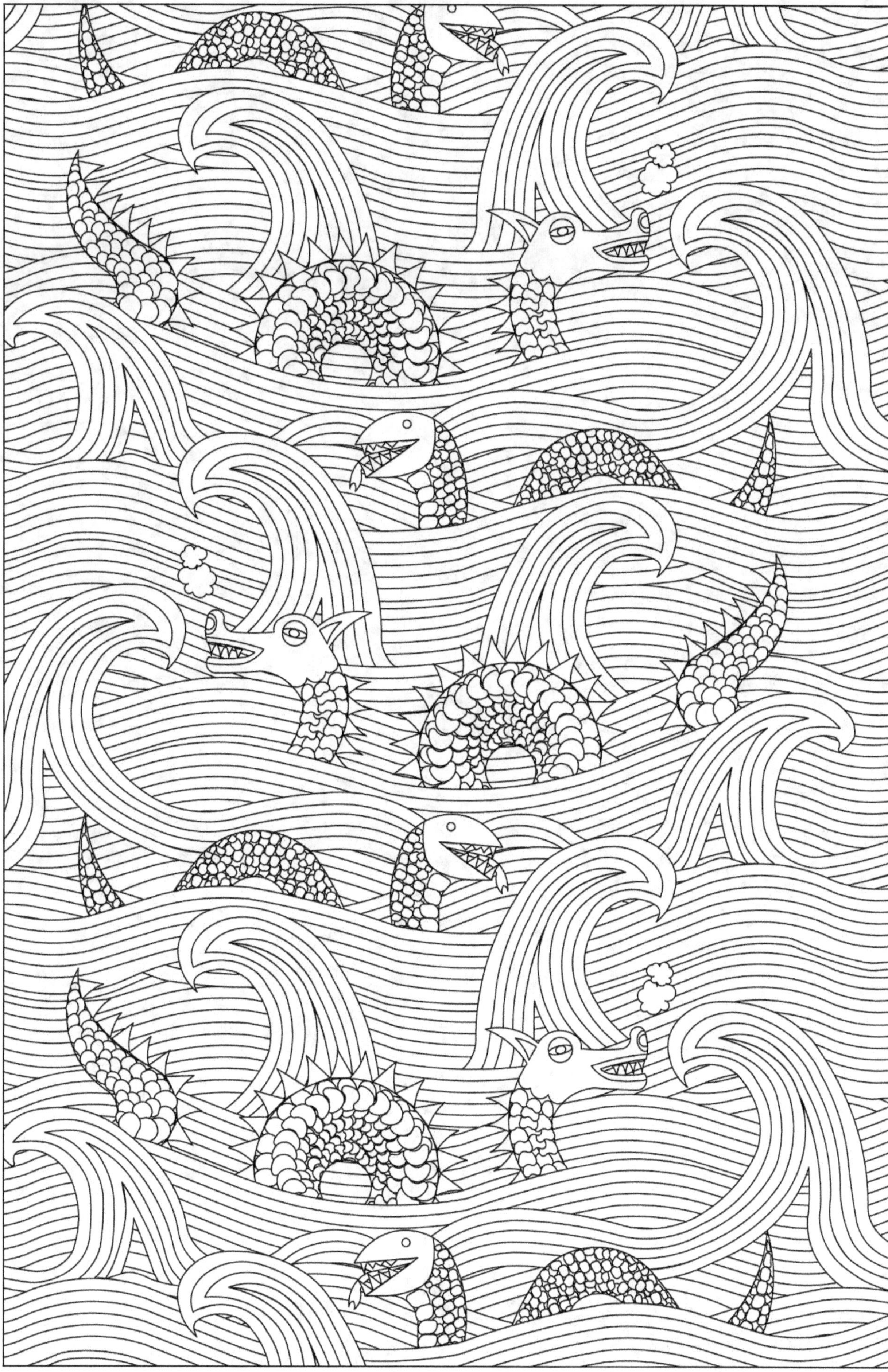

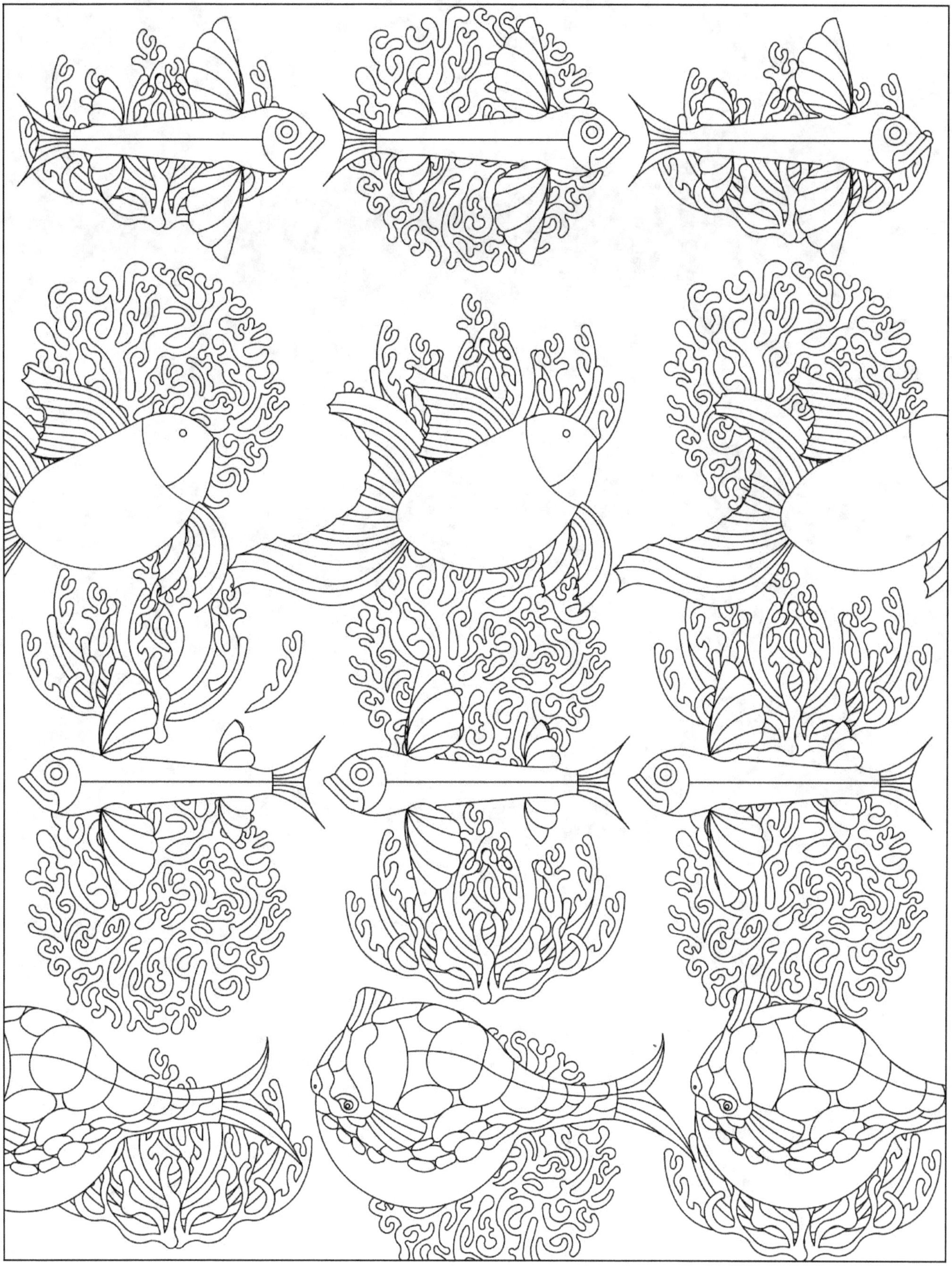

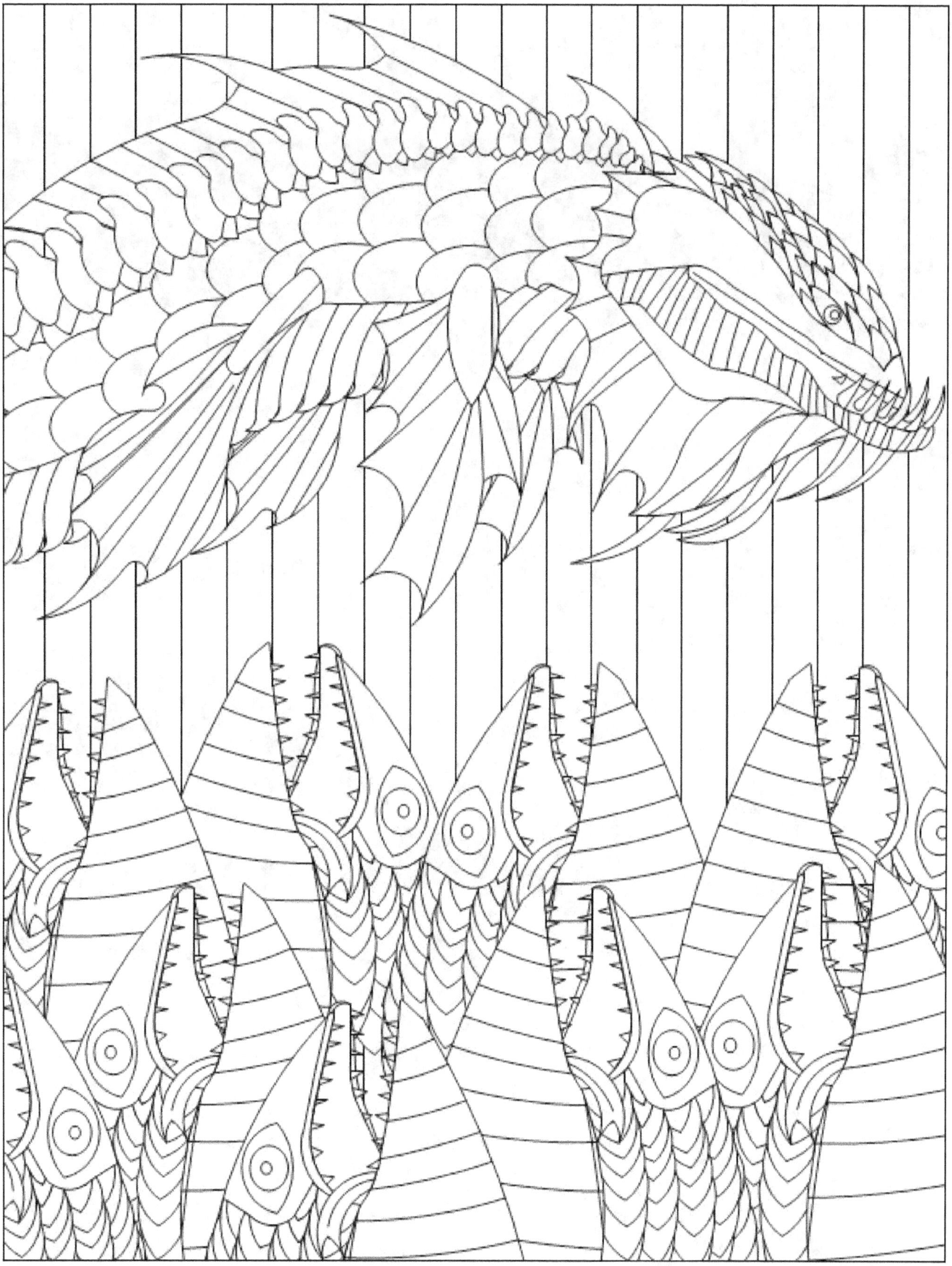

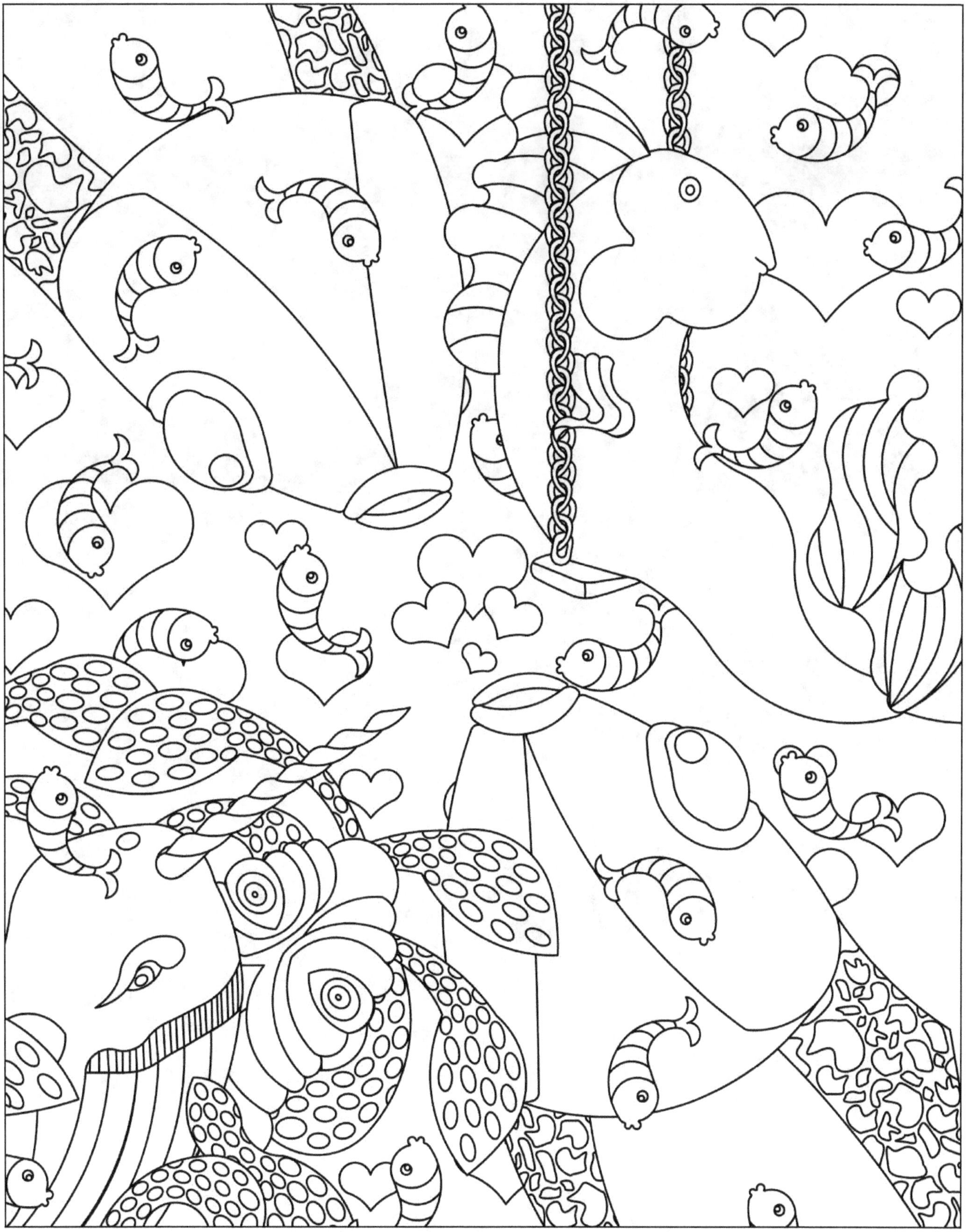

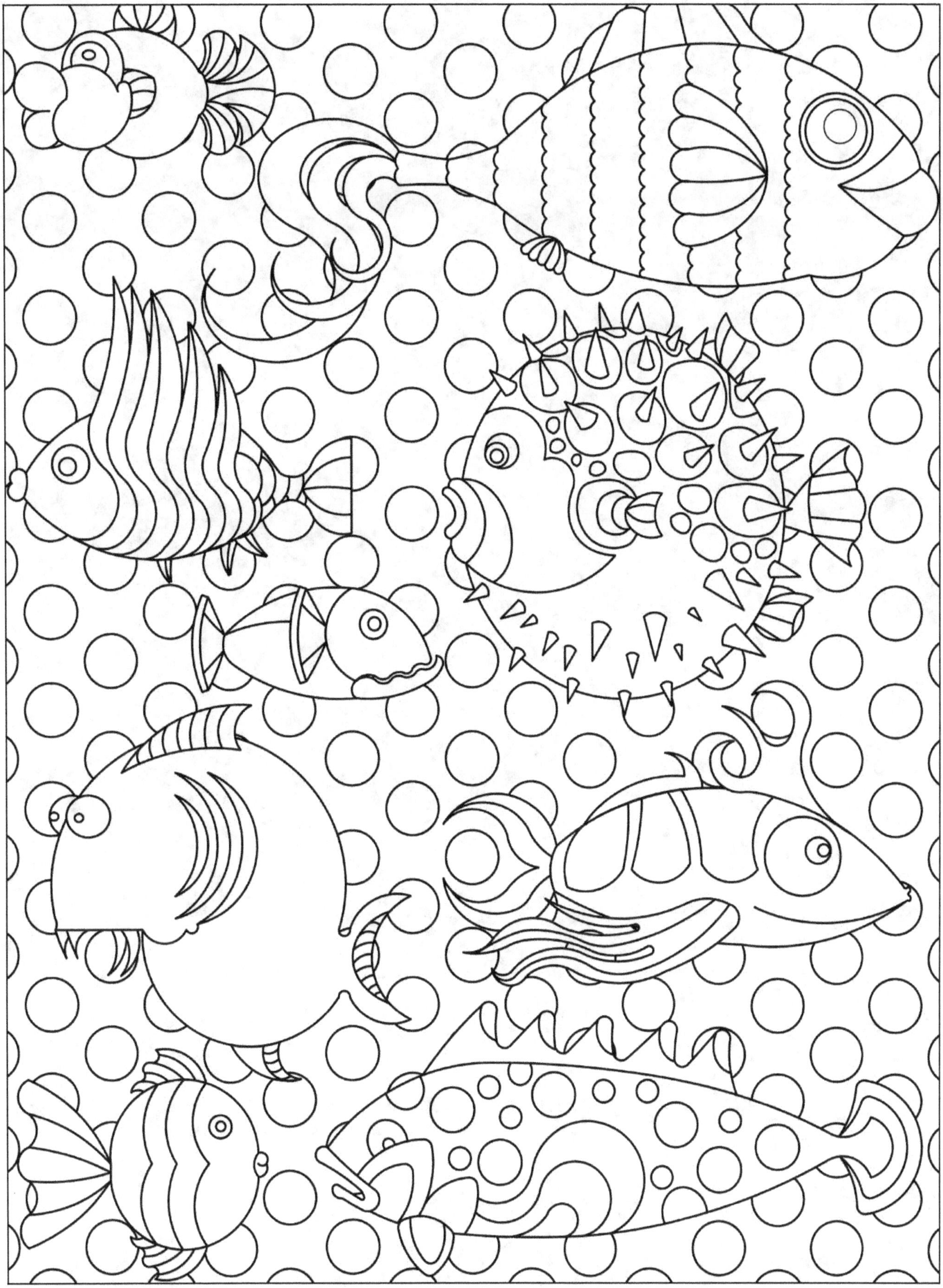

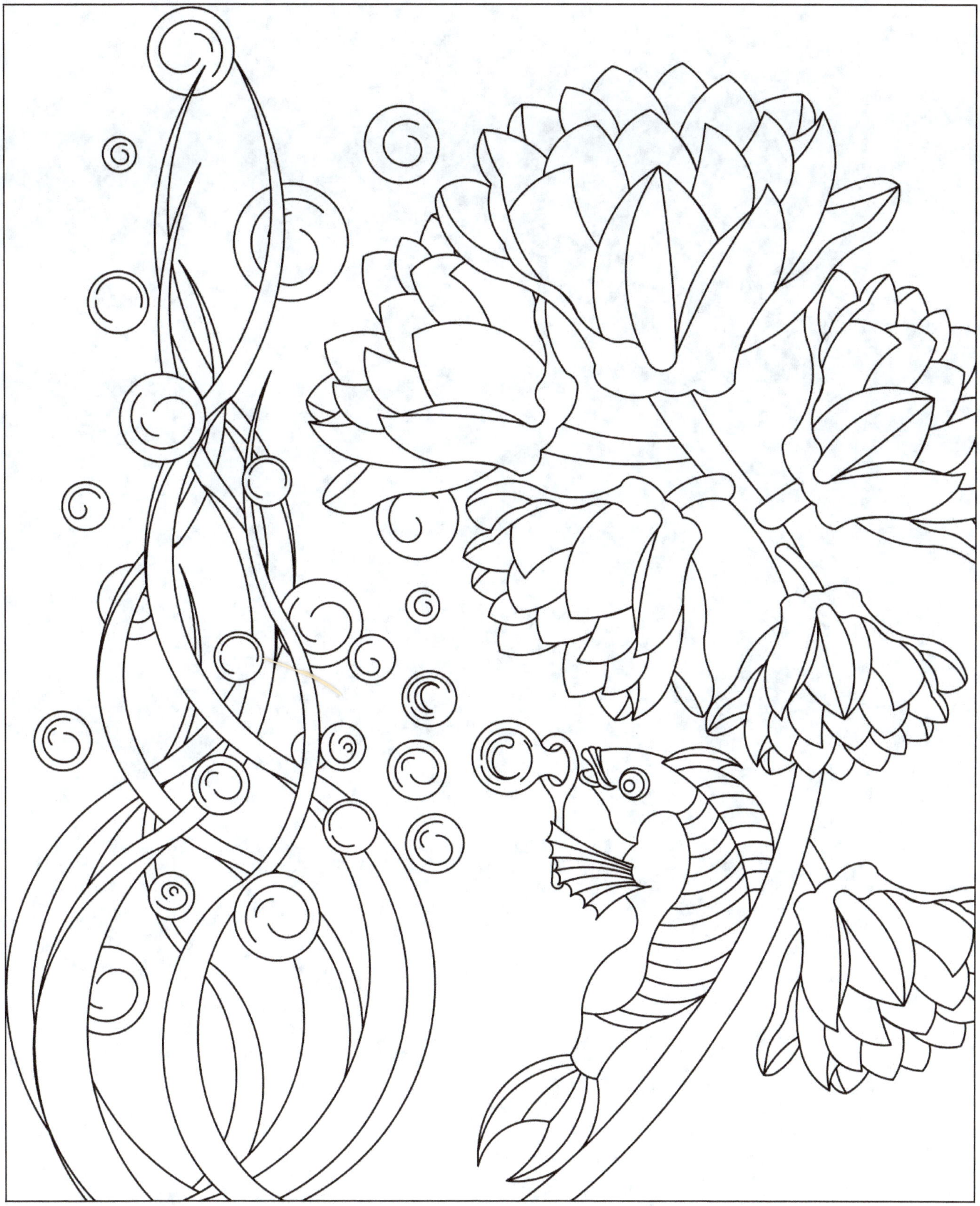

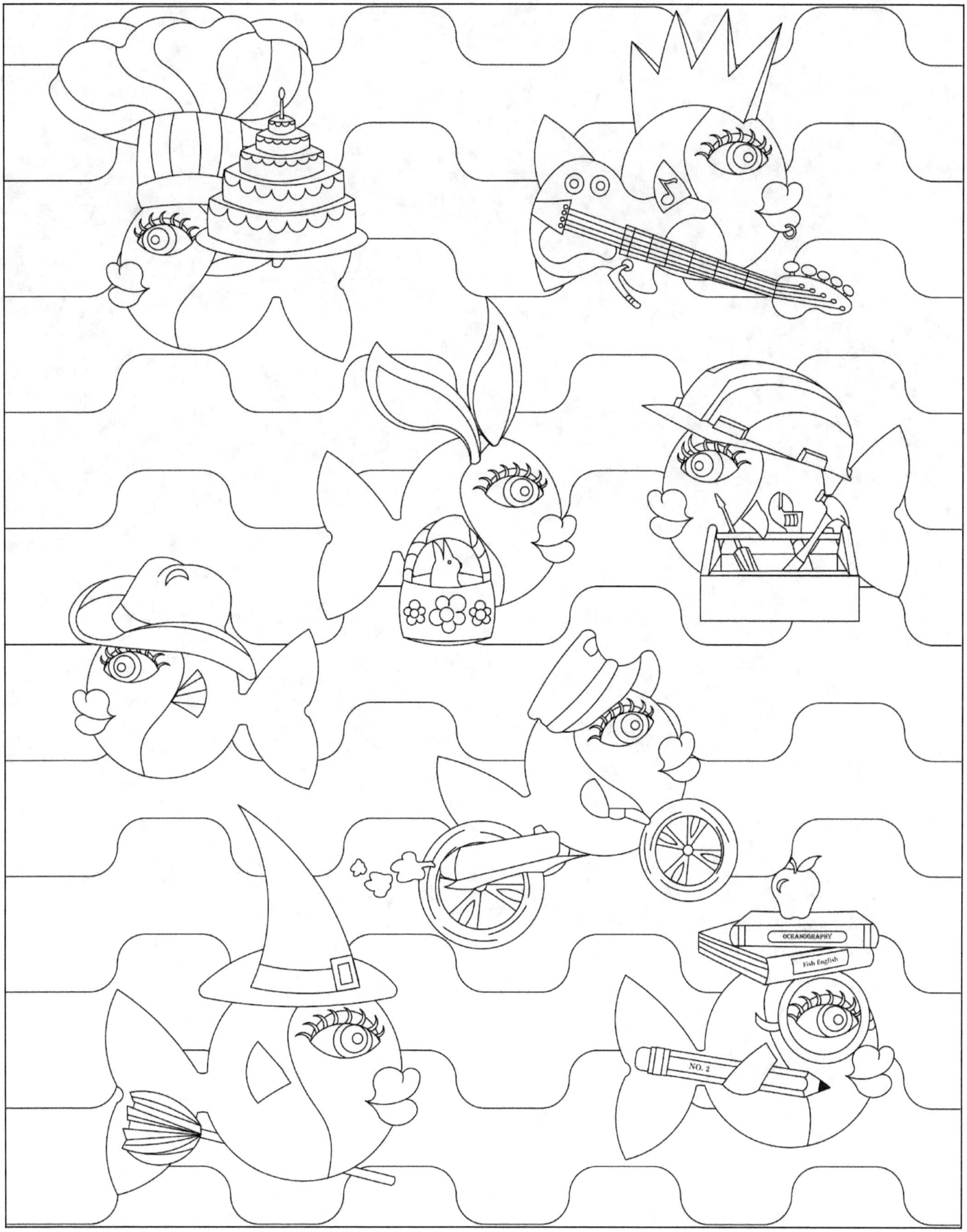
OCEANOGRAPHY
Fish English
NO. 2

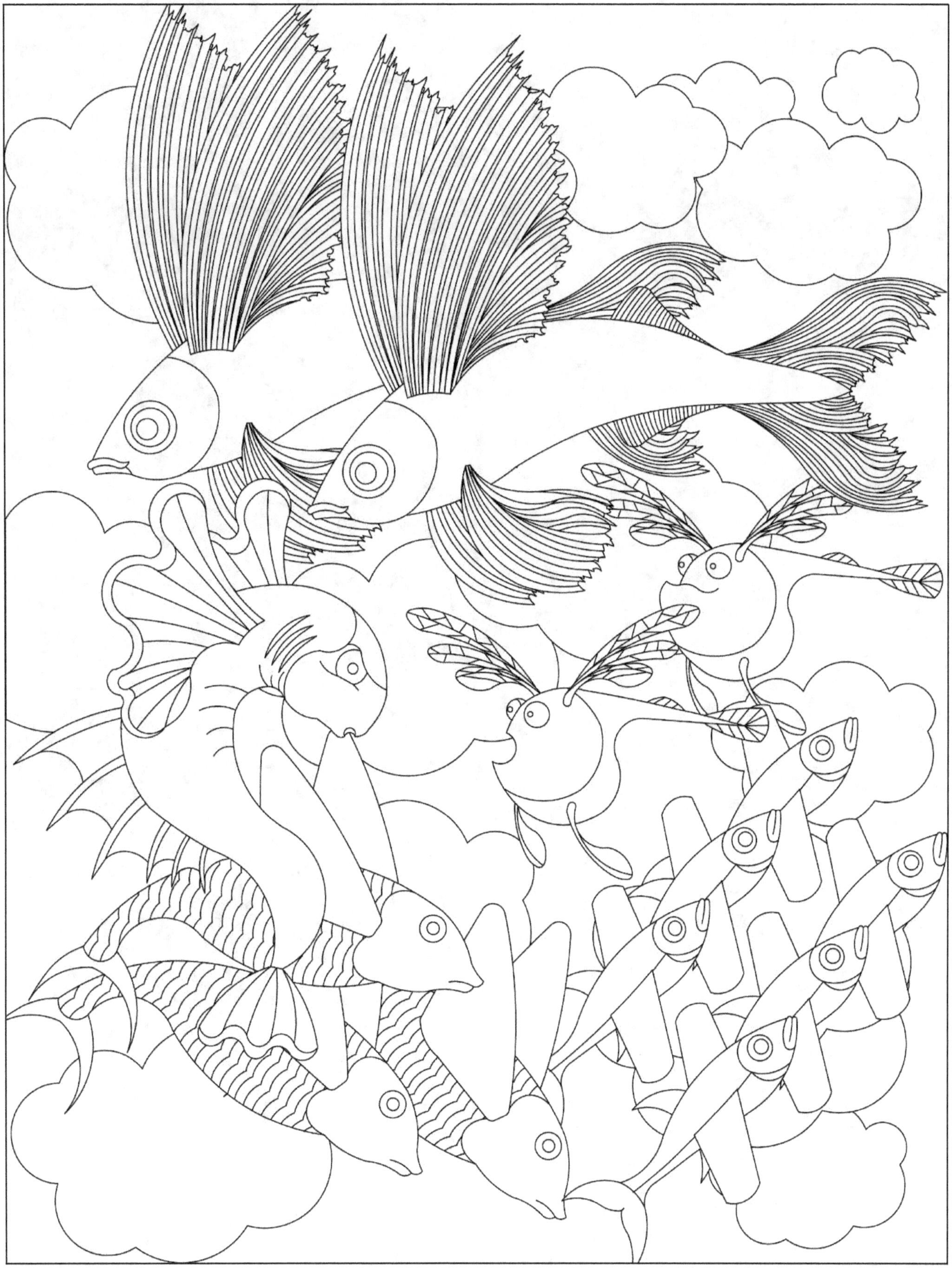

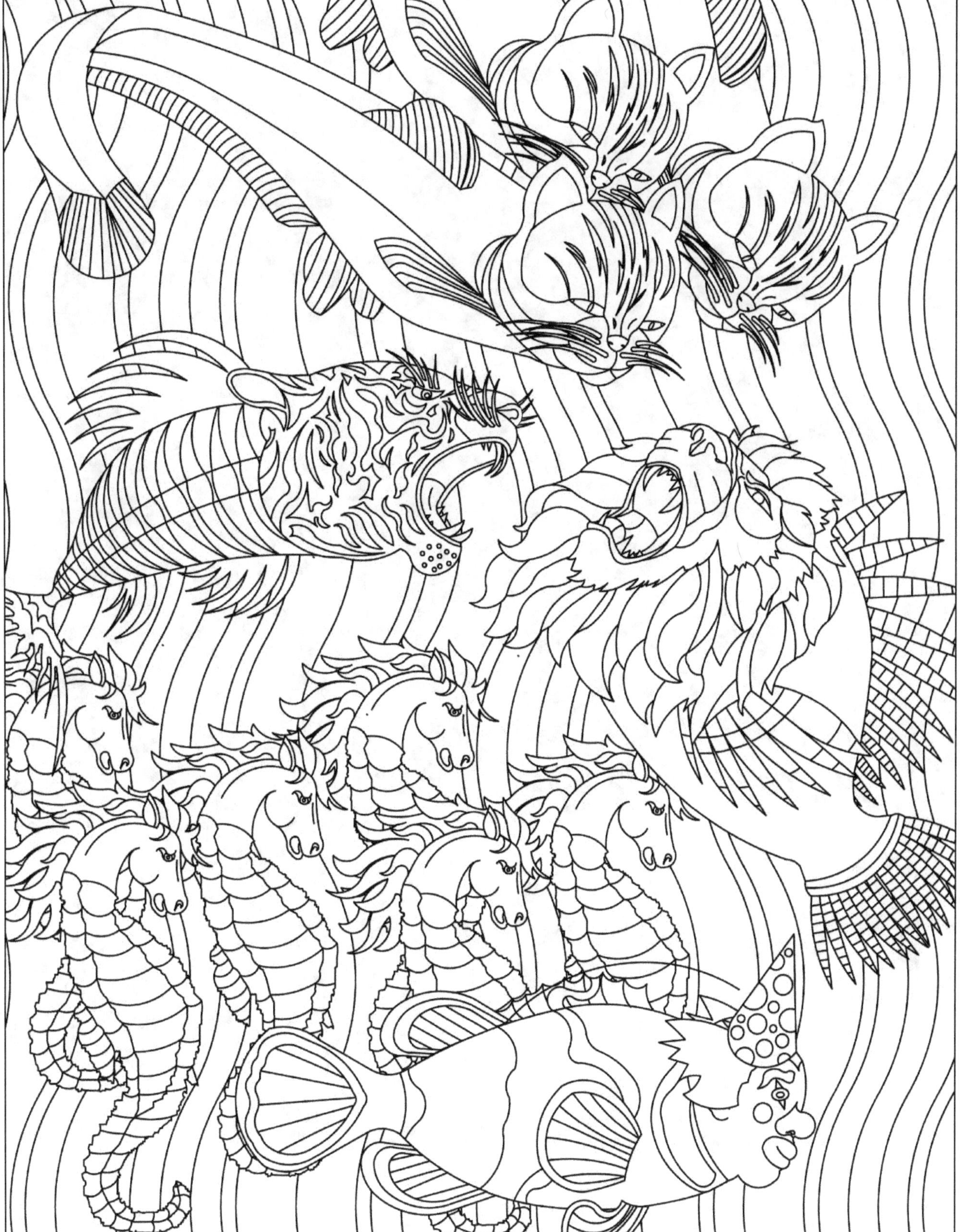

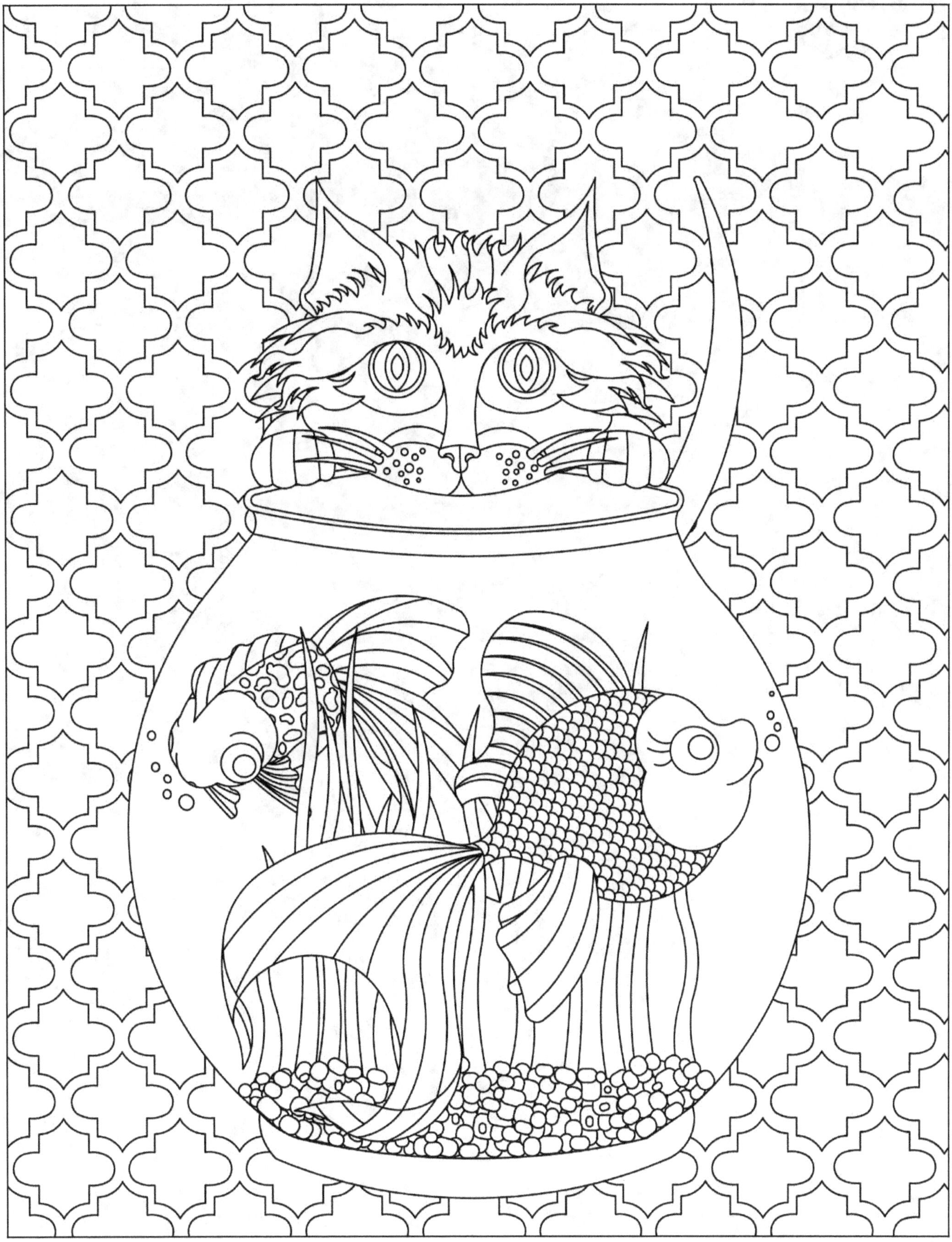

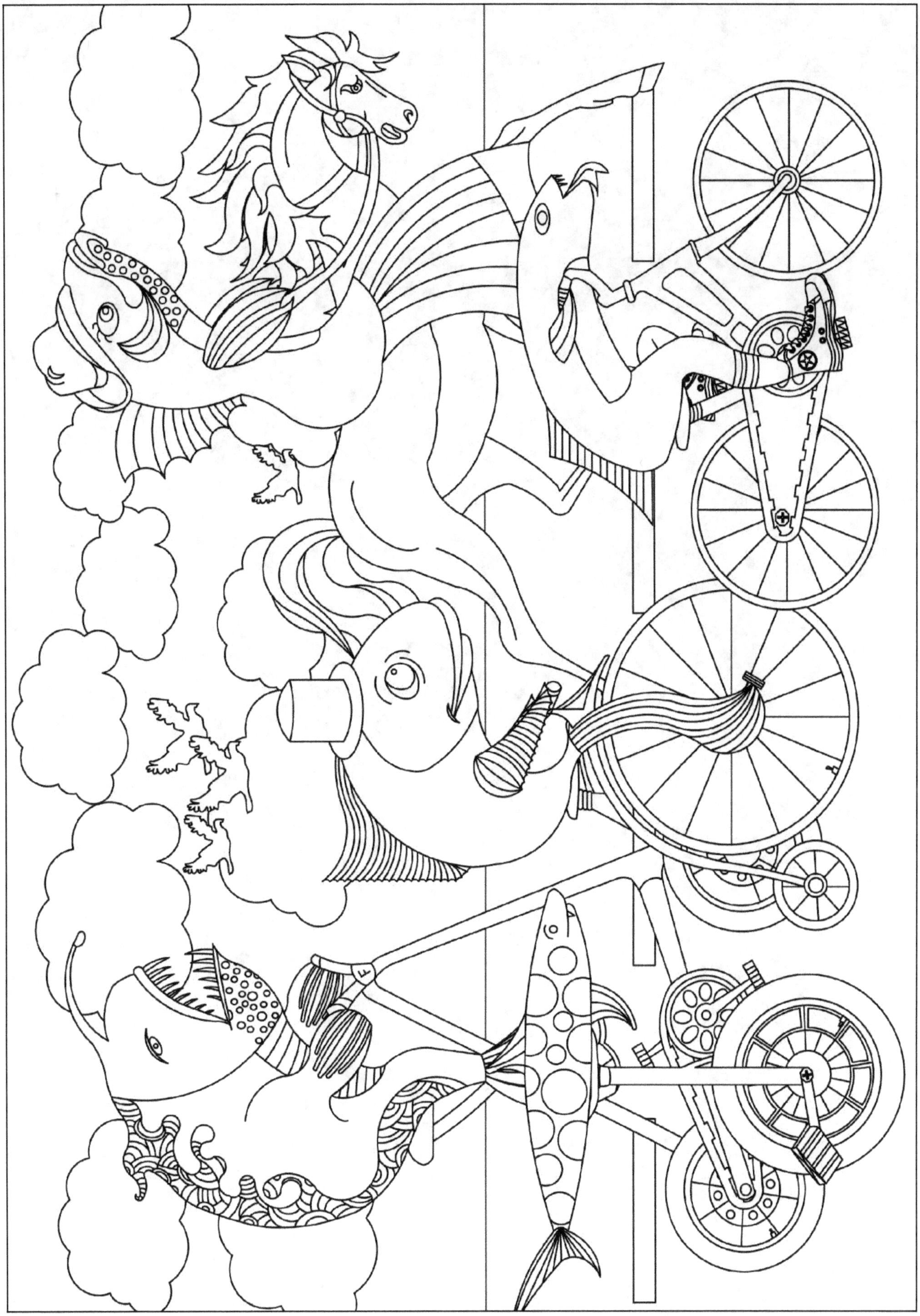

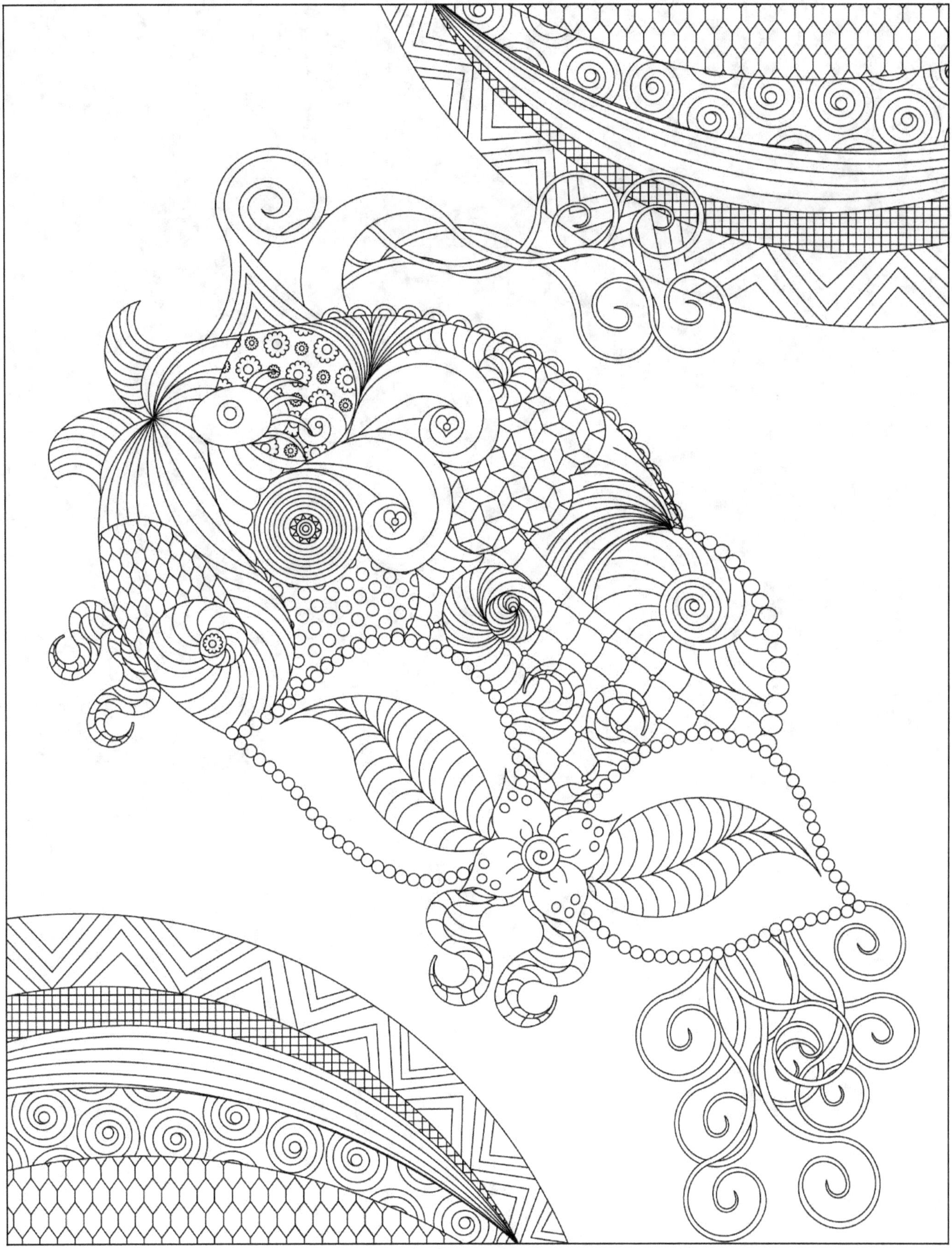

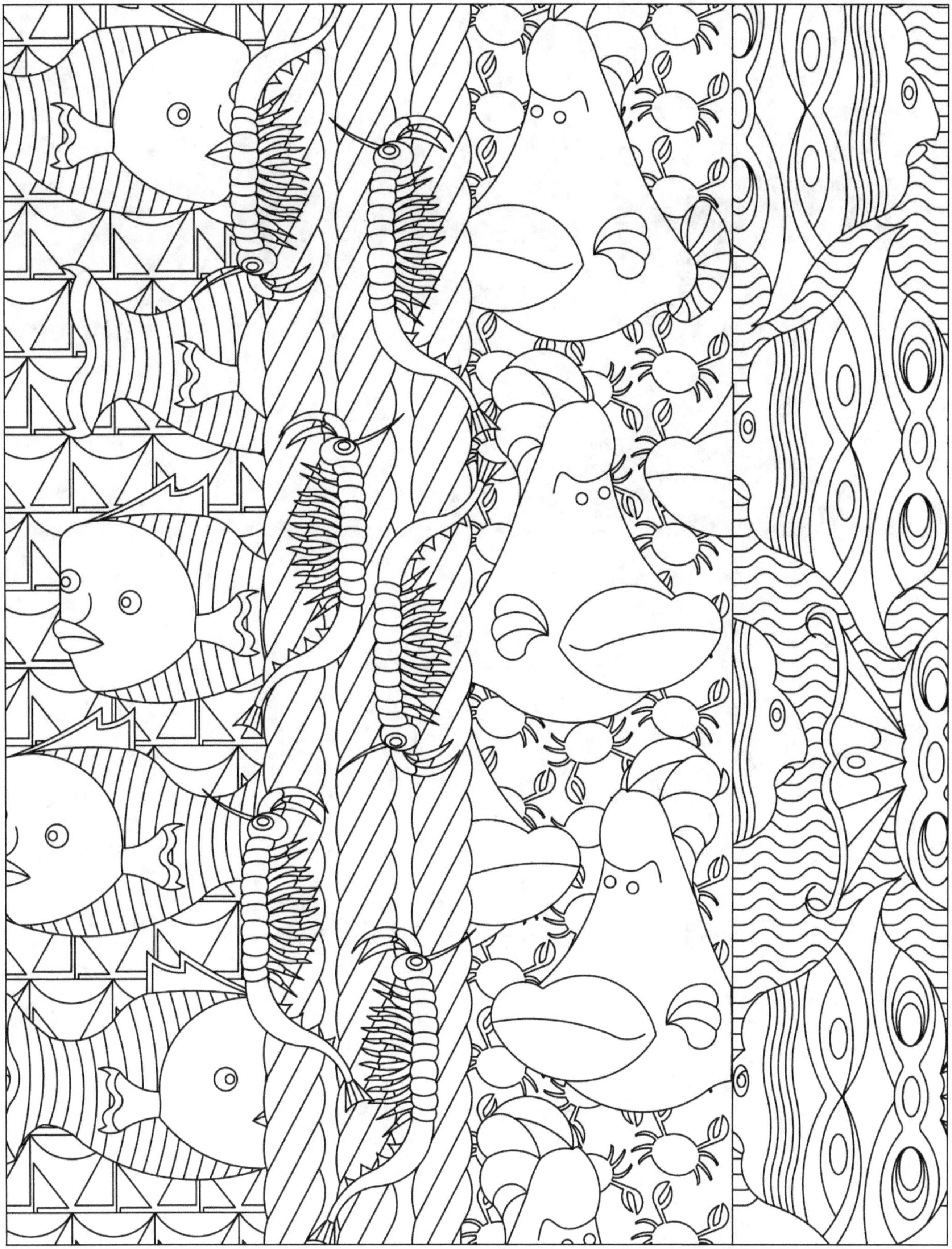

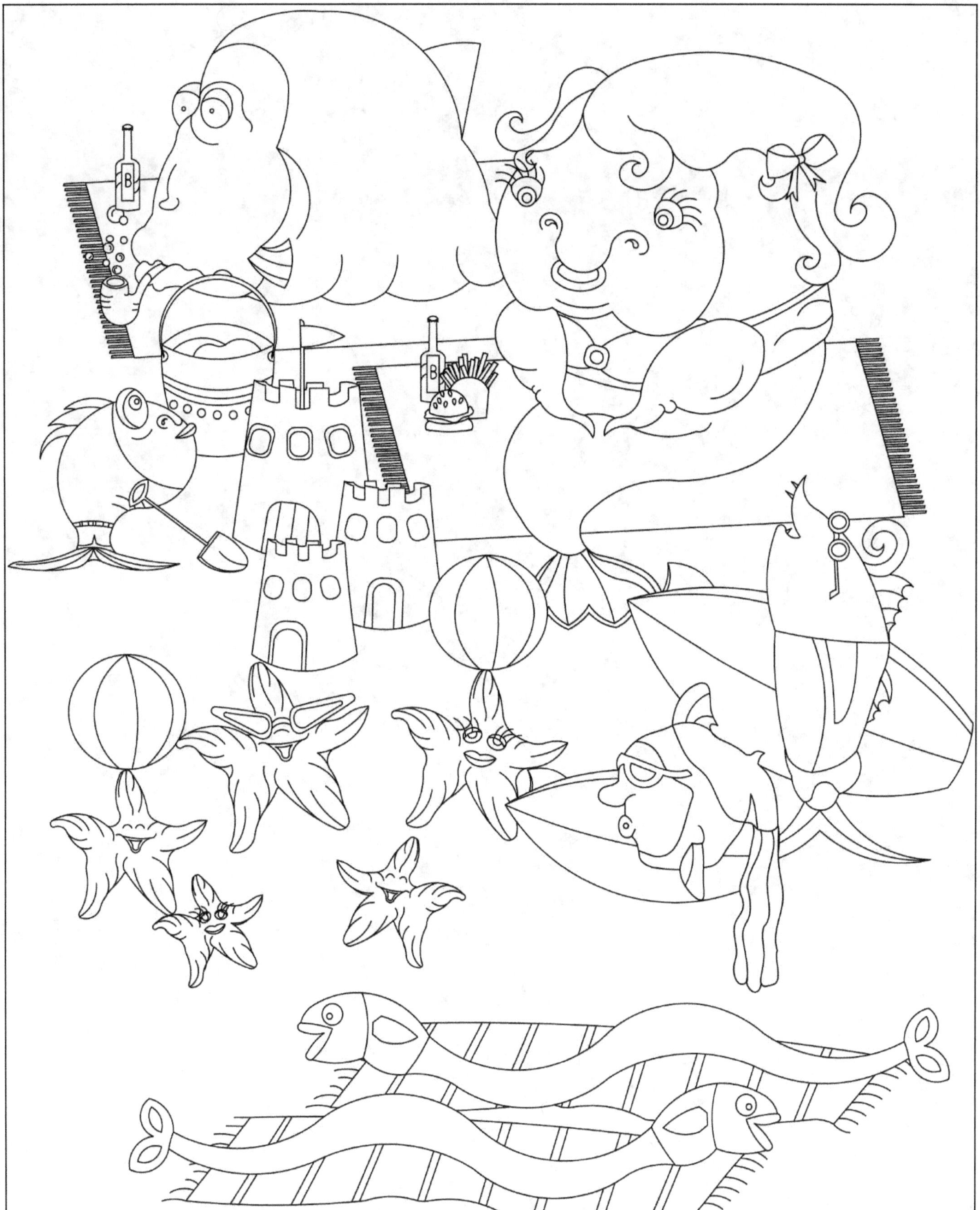

www.ingramcontent.com/pod-product-compliance
Lightning Source LLC
Chambersburg PA
CBHW081257180526
45170CB00007B/2461